Collins
ABC
Dictionary

Collins ABC Dictionary

Written by Irene Yates
Illustrated by Chris Fisher
Consultant Editor: Ginny Lapage

Collins

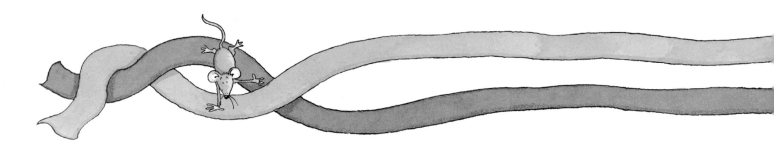

Managing Editor: Jilly MacLeod
Art Director: Rachel Hamdi
Design Consultant: Sophie Stericker
Cover Designer: Nicola Croft
Designers: Holly Mann, Sarah Borny
Editor: Mary O'Riordan

First published in 2005 by Collins

© HarperCollins*Publishers* Ltd 2005

Published by Collins
a division of HarperCollins*Publishers* Ltd
77-85 Fulham Palace Road, London W6 8JB

www.collins.co.uk

Browse the complete Collins Education catalogue at:
www.collinseducation.com

ISBN 0 00 720348 9

10 9 8 7 6 5 4 3 2

Printed by Printing Express Ltd, Hong Kong

Contents

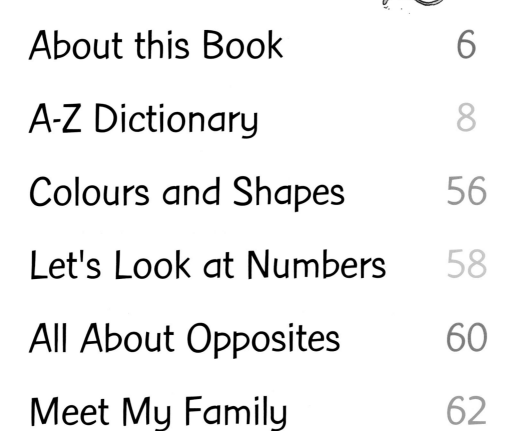

How to Use this Book

rabbit

This delightful book is full of humour and funny illustrations. But its serious aim is to help develop early language and literacy skills. To get the most out of it, sit with your child and talk and laugh about what you see – look at the letters, answer the questions, and giggle at the pictures together.

Read, Read and Re-read

Come back to the book over and over again, to expand your child's vocabulary and teach valuable dictionary and alphabetical skills.

crocodile

Read the alphabet together frequently, pointing to each letter as you go. Soon your child will begin to absorb its rhythm.

Encourage your child to trace these big letters with a finger. Say the names of the capitals, and make the sounds of the lower-case letters.

Look for the animals and ideas illustrated here elsewhere on the spread.

Read this sentence out loud, emphasizing its alliteration. Help your child to say the words.

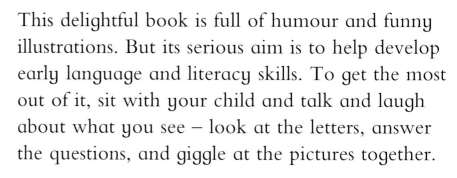

ear
The rabbit has long **ears**.

earth
Our home is on the **earth**.

eat
The dog likes to **eat** spaghetti.

The elephant exercises on an egg.

dog

Help your child learn the letter names and the letter sounds. Encourage them to match words to pictures, and words to words (see below), which are key skills for learning to read.

The Characters

A key feature of this dictionary is the hilarious animal characters shown here and throughout the book. Look for favourite characters to see what they're up to. Also look for favourite pictures and read the words associated with them. Above all, encourage your child to talk about the characters and everything else they see.

the mice

mummy and baby bear

elephant

Encourage your child to match the headword to the picture and to the word in bold type in the sentence (word to word matching).

These sentences give plenty of scope for talk. Ask the questions and make up more of your own, avoiding questions that only require "yes" or "no" as an answer.

Talk about what's happening in the picture. Help your child to identify what's going on with events in their own life.

egg
Who's that climbing out of his **egg**?

elephant
The **elephant** is as big as a bus.

engine
The **engine** makes the car go.

astic
ee how far the **astic** will stretch.

empty
Oh dear! The bottle is **empty**.

exercise
We **exercise** to keep fit.

ows
st on my **elbows** ead my book.

end
The **end** of the story. Time for bed!

eyes
How many **eyes** do you have?

A B C D E F G H I J K L M
a b c d e f g h i j k l m

The alligator is asleep in his aeroplane.

address

My **address** is where I live.

Roland Rabbit
78 Buckwheat Burrows
Dingley Down

aeroplane

Look who's flying the **aeroplane**.

alien

This **alien** comes from outer space.

N O P Q R S T U V W X Y Z
n o p q r s t u v w x y z

alligator
The **alligator** likes to bathe in mud.

animal
What kind of **animal** is this?

arm
Are your **arms** very strong?

alphabet
Have you learnt your **alphabet** yet?

ankle
My **ankle** joins my foot to my leg.

asleep
Grandad snores when he's **asleep**.

angry
Grrr! The bear is getting very **angry!**

apple
This **apple** is good to eat.

awake
The mouse is wide **awake**. Are you?

Bb

The bear blows
up a balloon on his bike.

baby

The **baby** makes an awful noise.

badge

Do you have a **badge** to wear?

balloon

Hang on tight to the **balloon**.

banana

Pick a **banana** from a tree.

bed

I've made my **bed** in a box.

blow

The elephant likes to **blow** bubbles.

bang

Fireworks make a loud **bang**.

bike

Riding a **bike** is lots of fun.

book

What is your favourite **book**?

bear

The **bear** lives in a cosy cave.

birthday

Whose **birthday** is it today?

butterfly

This **butterfly** has beautiful wings.

ABCDEFGHIJKLM
abcdefghijklm

Cc

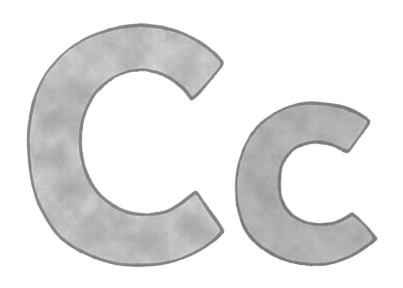

The cat catches
a cake in her cap.

cake
That **cake** looks delicious!

candle
Count the **candles** on the cake.

cap
Do you wear your **cap** back to front?

car

The crocodile drives a shiny red **car**.

cat

Time for supper, says the **cat**.

chick

One day, the **chicks** will grow into hens.

carrot

Look at my big tasty **carrot**.

catch

The dog tries to **catch** the ball.

chocolate

Do you like **chocolate**, too?

castle

Let's build a **castle** out of sand.

caterpillar

This **caterpillar** is very hairy.

chopsticks

The rabbit eats with **chopsticks**.

A B C D E F G H I J K L M
a b c d e f g h i j k l m

Cc

cloud
The sun is hiding behind a **cloud**.

computer
The rabbit plays on her **computer**.

clock
What time does the **clock** say?

cobweb
A spider made this pretty **cobweb**.

count
Count to ten with the bear.

clothes
I like dressing up in funny **clothes**.

colour
Red is my favourite **colour**.

crab
Ouch! That **crab** has sharp claws.

crane

Which is taller – the **crane** or the house?

cup

The mouse drinks his juice from a **cup**.

cutting

Do you like **cutting** and sticking, too?

crocodile

The **crocodile** has big pointed teeth.

cry

Please don't make the elephant **cry**.

The crocodile counts
clocks in the clouds.

15

Dd

The dog dances
with a dinosaur.

dance

Do you like to
dance?

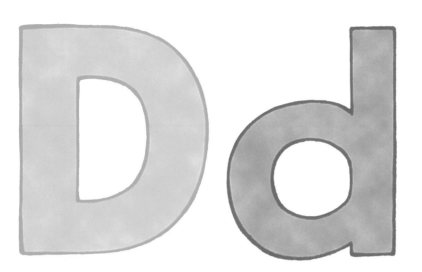

dentist

The **dentist** looks
after our teeth.

different

What's **different**
about these bears?

dig

How many bones does the dog **dig** up?

dog

The **dog** wags his tail with delight.

drop

Don't **drop** the apples!

dinosaur

This **dinosaur** lived a very long time ago.

dragon

Watch out! That **dragon** is fierce!

drum

The crocodile beats his **drum**.

doctor

Poor bear is ill. Send for the **doctor**!

drink

What's your favourite **drink**?

duck

Mother **duck** looks after her ducklings.

A B C D **E** F G H I J K L M
a b c d **e** f g h i j k l m

E e

The elephant
exercises on an egg.

ear

The rabbit has very
long **ears**.

earth

Our home is on
the **earth**.

eat

The dog likes to
eat spaghetti.

egg

Who's that climbing out of his **egg**?

elephant

The **elephant** is as big as a bus.

engine

The **engine** makes the car go.

elastic

See how far the **elastic** will stretch.

empty

Oh dear! The bottle is **empty**.

exercise

We **exercise** to keep fit.

elbows

I rest on my **elbows** to read my book.

end

The **end** of the story. Time for bed!

eyes

How many **eyes** do you have?

A B C D E F G H I J K L M
a b c d e f g h i j k l m

Ff

The farmer is
frightened by the frog.

face

Do you have freckles
on your **face**?

farmer

The **farmer** has a
big red tractor.

feather

Poor bird! She's lost
a **feather**.

feet
Our **feet** are made for walking.

flower
This **flower** smells lovely.

frog
See how far the **frog** can jump.

fire engine
A **fire engine** rushes to the fire.

friend
Who is your best **friend**?

fun
This slide is lots of **fun**.

fish
The **fish** swim in the pond.

frightened
The boy is very **frightened**!

funny
Ha ha! Doesn't the bear look **funny**?

A B C D E F **G** H I J K L M

Gg

The giant gives
a giraffe some grapes.

game
What **game** shall
we play today?

gate
Quick! Close the
gate behind you.

giant
Here comes the
giant. Run!

22

giraffe

The **giraffe** has a long, long neck.

go

Ready, steady, **go**! Who'll win the race?

greedy

Don't be **greedy**! Leave some for us.

give

Give the elephant a big present.

good

The dog is **good** at drawing. Are you?

grow

Do you **grow** taller every year?

glue

Glue is good for sticking things.

grapes

Look who's eating all the **grapes**.

grumpy

The bear is feeling **grumpy**.

The happy hippopotamus
flies his helicopter.

hair

How long is your
hair?

hammer

Hit the nail in with
a **hammer**.

hands

We wave our **hands**
to say goodbye.

happy
The elephant is **happy** with his toy.

heavy
That bag is too **heavy** to carry.

hot
Don't touch that. It's **hot**.

hat
Which **hat** do you like best?

helicopter
Up, up and away in the **helicopter**.

house
What does your **house** look like?

hear
Listen! Can you **hear** the music?

hippopotamus
The **hippopotamus** lives in the water.

hug
Give me a nice big **hug**.

A B C D E F G H I J K L M
a b c d e f g h i j k l m

Ii

The insect
juggles with ice cream.

ice cream
Don't let the **ice cream** melt.

ill
Stay in bed if you feel **ill**.

indoors
Oh dear! We'll have to play **indoors**.

Jj

insect

How many legs does an **insect** have?

iron

The elephant likes to **iron** his shirts.

island

Welcome to my **island** in the sun.

jacket

Do you like my new **jacket**?

jigsaw

Find the missing piece of **jigsaw**.

juggle

The crocodile likes to **juggle**.

jump

I can **jump** higher than you.

Kk

kangaroo

This **kangaroo** has a baby in her pouch.

ketchup

I like **ketchup** with everything.

key

See if the **key** fits the lock.

The kangaroo
gives the king a kiss.

kick

Kick the ball into the net.

kite

The **kite** flies high in the sky.

knife

Be careful with that **knife**. It's sharp.

king

The **king** wears a golden crown.

kitten

The **kitten** loves to play with string.

know

Do you **know** a spaceman?

kiss

Give me a **kiss** to show you love me.

knee

Bounce the baby on your **knee**.

koala

A **koala** eats leaves up in the trees.

L l

The lamb laughs at
the lion on the ladder.

ladder

See how high the **ladder** goes.

ladybird

Count the spots on the **ladybird**.

lamb

A **lamb** is a baby sheep.

laugh
We all **laugh** at the funny dog.

letter
The crocodile posts his **letter**.

look
The birds **look** for worms to eat.

leaf
The caterpillar munches on a **leaf**.

lid
Quick! Close the **lid** on the box.

loud
That music is too **loud**. Turn it down!

leg
Can you stand on one **leg**, too?

lion
Hear the mighty **lion** roar.

RRRR!

love
Who do you **love** best?

A B C D E F G H I J K L **M**
a b c d e f g h i j k l **m**

M m

The mice make
a music machine.

machine
What does this
machine make?

make
Let's **make** a cake
for tea.

mask
Guess who's wearing
a scary **mask**.

medicine
Take your **medicine**.
It'll make you better.

mirror
It's fun making
faces in a **mirror**.

monster
Are you scared of
the **monster**?

middle
Look who's standing
in the **middle**.

money
The dog has saved
lots of **money**.

mouse
One **mouse** here.
Two mice there.

milk shake
I like to drink **milk
shake**. Do you?

monkey
What's the **monkey**
up to now?

music
The animals make
music together.

name
My **name** is on my hat.

naughty
The mice are being very **naughty**.

neck
My **neck** holds my head on.

The newt puts numbers in his nest.

needle

The rabbit sews with a **needle** and thread.

new

Look who's bought a **new** hat.

nose

We smell things with our **nose**.

nest

How many eggs are in the **nest**?

newt

The **newt** likes to eat eggs.

nothing

Oh no! There's **nothing** left to eat.

net

Let's catch some fish in a **net**.

noise

Stop that **noise**. It's terrible!

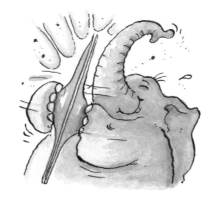

number

What **number** am I holding?

a b c d e f g h i j k l m

O o

The ostrich
jumps over the octopus.

oak tree
The **oak tree** grows from an acorn.

o'clock
It's seven **o'clock**. Time to get up.

octopus
The **octopus** has eight tentacles.

often

How **often** do you change your socks?

opposite

What's the **opposite** of thin?

outside

Let's go **outside** and play.

old

This teddy bear is very **old**.

orange

Peel the **orange** before you eat it.

over

Whoops! The rabbit has fallen **over**.

open

Open the door to see who's there.

ostrich

Have you ever seen an **ostrich** fly?

owl

The **owl** hunts for food at night.

A B C D E F G H I J K L M
a b c d e f g h i j k l m

P p

The panda pulls the penguin out of the puddle.

paint
Paint a picture of your house.

panda
The **panda** likes to eat bamboo.

parcel
Who is this big **parcel** for?

For You.

pattern
The dog paints a **pattern** on his face.

penguin
The **penguin** lives in a cold, snowy place.

pizza
Mmm! **Pizza** is my favourite food.

peas
How do you eat your **peas**?

pet
Do you have a **pet** of your own?

play
Let's all **play** hide-and-seek.

pencil
I can write my name with a **pencil**.

picture
Clever rabbit! He's drawn a **picture**.

postman
The **postman** brings the letters.

Pp

promise

Will you **promise** to be good?

puppy

Oh dear! Look what the **puppy** has done.

present

Here's a **present** for your birthday.

puddle

Splish, splash, splosh in the **puddle**.

push

Give the elephant a big **push**!

pretty

Molly looks **pretty** in her new dress.

pull

Pull! **Pull**! As hard as you can.

pyjamas

Get your **pyjamas** on, ready for bed.

Q q

quiet

Keep **quiet**. You'll wake the baby.

quack

Hear the ducks go **quack**, **quack**!

quick

Be **quick**, or you'll be late for school.

queen

Oh no! The **queen** has lost her crown.

Quick! Keep the queen quiet.

ABCDEFGHIJKLM
abcdefghijklm

Rr

The rabbit races
against the robot.

rabbit
What's the **rabbit**
doing now?

race
Who is going to win
the **race**?

rainbow
Look at the **rainbow**
in the sky.

42

read

The bear is learning to **read**. Are you?

ride

Can you **ride** a bicycle yet?

rocket

Blastoff! The **rocket** shoots into space.

rhinoceros

The **rhinoceros** has sharp horns.

ring

Wow! Look how the **ring** sparkles.

row

The mice line up in a **row**.

ribbon

Tie the parcel up with **ribbon**.

robot

Let the **robot** do all the work.

run

I can **run** faster than you!

S s

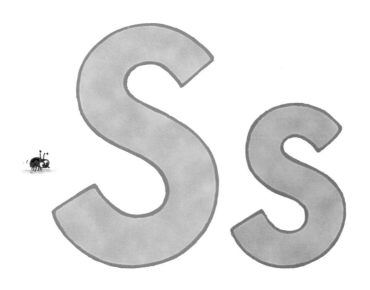

sad

Poor elephant is feeling **sad**.

sausage

That **sausage** looks very tasty!

scissors

Cut out the picture with the **scissors**.

The snake sings
on her skateboard.

44

shadow

Can you stamp on your **shadow**?

shell

There are lots of **shells** on the beach.

skateboard

The dog whizzes by on his **skateboard**.

shampoo

We wash our hair with **shampoo**.

shoes

Those **shoes** look too big!

smile

Give me a nice big **smile**.

shape

Tell me what **shape** this is.

sing

Let's all **sing** "Three Blind Mice".

snail

The **snail** is a terrible slowcoach.

45

soap

Wash your face with **soap** and water.

spider

How many legs does a **spider** have?

snake

Watch out! That **snake** is poisonous!

spade

The dog is digging with his **spade.**

spoon

We eat our ice cream with a **spoon**.

snowball

Let's have a **snowball** fight.

spaghetti

Spaghetti is great fun to eat.

squirrel

The **squirrel** is burying his nuts.

N O P Q R **S** T U V W X Y Z

n o p q r **s** t u v w x y z

story
Please read me a bedtime **story**.

swim
The crocodile likes to **swim**. Do you?

swing
Make the **swing** go way up high.

strawberry
Mmm! **Strawberry** jam is my favourite.

strong
The elephant is very **strong**.

The spider throws snowballs at the squirrel.

T t

The tiger eats his toast under the table.

table

We sit at the **table** to eat our tea.

tail

See who has the longest **tail**.

teeth

Do you brush your **teeth** every day?

television

Let's all watch **television**.

toast

That **toast** looks very tasty.

train

The **train** chugs along the track.

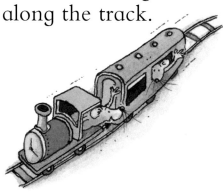

thumb

Poor dog has hurt his **thumb**. Ouch!

toe

Sam can touch his **toes**. Can you?

tree

Look who is stuck in the **tree**!

tiger

The **tiger** is a big fierce cat.

toy

Everyone likes to play with **toys**.

trumpet

Who is that playing the **trumpet**?

U u

The unicorn is under the umbrella.

ugly
Do you think the monster is **ugly**?

umbrella
It's raining. Open up your **umbrella**.

under
Look who's crawling **under** the fence.

unicorn

The **unicorn** is a magical beast.

upside down

It's fun hanging **upside down**.

vase

Put the flowers in the **vase**.

video

Which **video** shall we watch?

upstairs

Take your toys **upstairs** to bed.

vegetables

I love to eat **vegetables**.

visit

Let's go and **visit** grandma.

A B C D E F G H I J K L M
a b c d e f g h i j k l m

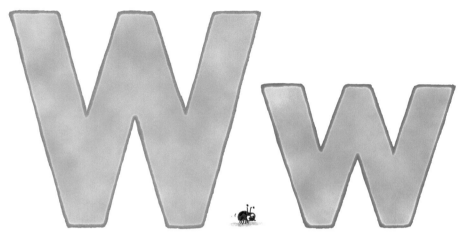

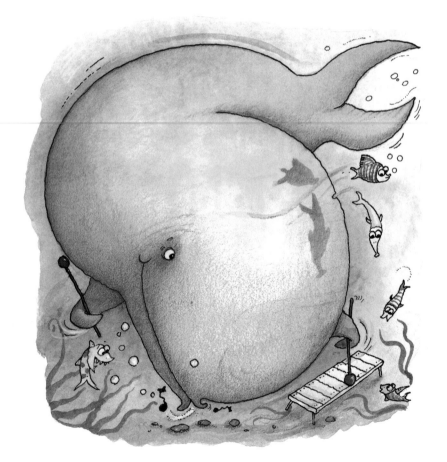

The whistling whale
plays the xylophone.

wash

Wash your face. It's very dirty!

watch

I use my **watch** to tell the time.

whale

The **whale** is an enormous animal.

X x

wheel

How many **wheels** does this bike have?

whistle

Blow the **whistle** to start the race.

window

What can you see through the **window**?

Xmas tree

Let's decorate the **Xmas tree**.

X-ray

An **X-ray** shows what's inside you.

xxxx

Write some **kisses** on your letter.

xylophone

The crocodile plays the **xylophone**.

A B C D E F G H I J K L M
a b c d e f g h i j k l m

Y y

The zebra eats
yogurt on his yacht.

yacht
A **yacht** has sails to
make it go.

yawn
That's a big **yawn**.
Guess who's tired.

year
I am one **year** old.
How old are you?

yogurt

Yummy! It's **yogurt** for breakfast!

yolk

This egg has two **yolks**!

zebra

The **zebra** has a stripy coat.

zip

Does your jacket fasten with a **zip**?

yo-yo

Watch me do tricks with my **yo-yo**.

zigzag

We can paint a **zigzag** pattern.

zoo

Let's go to the **zoo** to see the animals.

Colours and ...

red clothes

yellow flower

grey elephant

purple grapes

blue alien

black and white panda

orange carrots

green crocodile

pink dress

brown bear

... Shapes

triangle

square

circle

cube

rectangle

oval

sphere

star

heart

diamond

cone

What colour are these shapes?

57

Let's Look at Numbers

1 one rabbit

2 two robots

3 three chicks

4 four dogs

5 five presents

6 six books

7 seven hats

8 eight mice

9 nine bananas

10 ten oranges

11
eleven balloons

16
sixteen ice creams

12
twelve cups

17
seventeen spoons

13
thirteen butterflies

18
eighteen pencils

14
fourteen carrots

19
nineteen ladybirds

15
fifteen apples

20
twenty chopsticks

All About Opposites

big

little

day

night

in

out

fat

thin

hard

soft

dry

wet

short

long

on

off

up

down

clean

dirty

fast

slow

Meet My Family

Grandpa

Grandma

Auntie Doris

Mum

Dad

brother James

sister Sally

This is me!

Grandad

Granny

Great Uncle Albert

Uncle Arthur

Auntie Maud

cousin George

cousin Henry

cousin Lucy

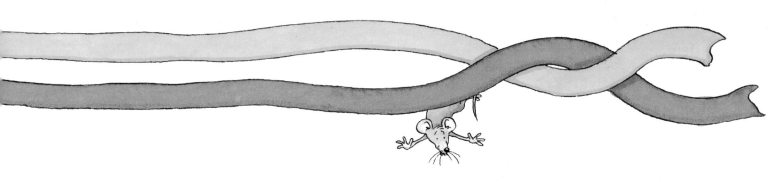

bye-bye!